How to Deal with Trials and

Spiritual Maturity

Bible Study in The Book of
James

By
William Guindi

Who is James the writer of the letter?

He is James, the brother of the Lord, as in (Gal 1:19). It is stated that the Lord Jesus has brothers in (Mt 13:55, 56), (Mk 6:3), and that one of his brothers is called James. There are other people in the New Testament by this name:
1- James son of Zebedee brother of John (Mt 4:21, 22), (Mk 3:17).
2- James son of Alphaeus (Mt 10:3), (Acts 1:13).
3- James (Lk 6:16)

But the author of this letter is not James the son of Zebedee, the brother of John, because King Herod had killed him by the sword in the year 44 A.D. (Acts 12:1, 2).

As for James son of Alphaeus, little is known about him, as in (Matthew 10:3, Acts 1:13), and there is no indication that this is the author of the letter. And the other James is also not the author of the letter.

James's Character

He must have been a profound spiritual person, even occupying the position of leader of the church in Jerusalem. He was not a believer in Christ during His earthly ministry (Jn 7:1-5), until the Lord appeared to him after His resurrection, as in (1 Cor 15:7).
When Peter was rescued from prison, he sent a private letter to James (Acts 12:17). And when Paul visited Jerusalem, he went into James, and told all the brethren all that God had done among the gentiles by his ministry (Acts 21: 18-19). And it was this James who presided over the

church conference in Jerusalem (Acts 15). Paul described him as a pillar of the church (Gal. 2:9). Tradition says that he was a man of prayer, and he used to pray on his knees until they got stiffened and hardened from kneeling a lot. It was also said that he was martyred in 62 A.D. by the Pharisees.

Who did James write to?
He wrote to Jews Believing in Christ, who were scattered. The period in which James led the church is considered a period of transition, so it is a difficult and critical period. There were many Christian Jews in Jerusalem who still adhered to the Old Testament law (Acts 21:20), the temple had its existence, and the ministry in the temple was not yet over. As for the full light of the gospel of God's grace, had not yet radiate its ray. They were saved by the blood of Christ, but they also lived under the law, seeking to go out into the glorious light of the rich grace of God according to the New Testament.

These Jews were rejected by the Gentiles, and when they became Christians, they also became rejected by their own people the Jews. The letter tells us that the majority of them were poor, and some of them suffered from the tyranny of the rich.

Why did James write to them?
Because they had problems in their personal and ecclesiastical lives:
1. Sin problems
2. Some believers were rich, and some were poor, and no one cared about them.
3. Church members competed for positions in the church, particularly teaching in the church.
4. Some have failed to live a life of faith in practice.
5. Tongue is not controlled.
6. Love of the world.

James quoted from the Old Testament, and he also made references to the words of the Lord Jesus, especially the Sermon on the Mount.

Comparisons between James and the words of the Lord Jesus in the Sermon on the Mount:

James 1:2	- And -	Matthew 5:10-12
James 1:4	- And -	Matthew 5:48
James 1:5	- And -	Matthew 7:7-12
James 1:22	- And -	Matthew 7:21-27
James 4:11-12	- And -	Matthew 7:1-5
James 5:1-3	- And -	Matthew 6:19-21

The Subject of the letter: Spiritual maturity
Key Message and Central Verse: "That you may be perfect and complete, without deficiencies in anything" (James 1:4).

Signs of a mature believer:
1. Patience in the test (James 1)
2. Live the Christian life in practice (James 2)
3. Control his tongue (James 3)
4. Peacemaker (James 4)
5. Praying in the tribulations (James 5)

Explanation of the book of James:

Chapter One

The first chapter contains three main ideas:
1. Victory in trials creates maturity (James 1:2-12)
2. How to deal with temptations and trials (James 1:13-18)
3. The dangers arising from self-deception (James 1:19-27)

First: Victory in trials creates maturity:
How to turn trials into victory (James 1:2-12)

No matter how harsh trials are, by faith we can triumph, and victory leads us to maturity. If we want to turn trials into victories, we have to obey four commands:
. Calculate
. Know
. Surrender
. Ask

In other words, there are four basic positions for victory in trials:
1. Fullness of joy
2. Understanding Thought
3. Surrendering the will to God
4. A heart open to faith

1. The attitude of being filled with joy
"Count it all joy ...." (James 1-2)
Jesus said, "In the world you will have tribulation, but trust, I have overcome the world" (Jn 16:33). The apostle Paul said: "It is by many tribulations that we should enter the kingdom of God" (Acts 14:22)

And the Apostle Peter says: "Beloved, do not be surprised by the burning affliction that is among you for the sake of your test, as if something strange befell you." (1 Pet 4:12)

Satan is fighting us, and the world is standing against us, and we are engaged in a spiritual battle that leads to various trials. But we must not look at the dark face of the situation, there is always the enlightening face, let us look at it and wait until God's work is completed in us.

Count it ..., in the sense of value, and the Apostle Paul knew how to calculate and evaluate things, after meeting with the Lord Jesus, he set new goals and priorities, and the things that were important in his life he counted them as waste. He said, "That I may gain Christ and be found in him" (Philippians 3:8).

Our example is Jesus Christ, who is written of Him, that "for the joy that is laid before Him, He endured the cross" (Heb 12:2).

Job knew how to count and evaluate, and he said, "For he knows my way, if he tempts me, I will come out like gold" (Job 23:10).

When trials come, we are to lift our hearts with thanksgiving to the Lord and be filled with joy because we have surrendered to the God in whom we trust and look at the trials with the eye of faith.

2. The attitude of understanding thought

"Knowing that the test of your faith creates patience" (James 1:3)

What does a Christian need to know, to make it easier for him or her when facing trials?

(1) Faith is always tested, and God tested Abraham.

(2) The test of faith is in our favor, not against us, and the word "test of your faith" means to certify and approve of your faith.

And the apostle Peter says: "That the purification of your faith, which is more precious than mortal gold, although it is tested by fire, it is for praise, honor, and glory at the revelation of Jesus Christ" (1 Pet 1:7).

Temptations work for the believer, not against him, and the apostle Paul says, "We know that all things work together for good, for those who love God who are called according to His purpose" (Rom 8:28). He also says that "the lightness of our temporal affliction creates for us more and more the weight of eternal glory" (2 Cor 4:17).

(3) Trials help us to mature:
God wants us to benefit from trials, gaining patience, endurance, and the ability to continue in life, as stated in (Rom 5:3-4) where he says: "We boast in tribulations, knowing that tribulation creates patience, and patience is purification, and acclamation is hope."

In Heb 10:36 it says, "For you need patience, so that if you do the will of God, you will receive the promise."

The path of trials is the only way in which God can teach us endurance, for endurance does not come from reading a book, or listening to a sermon, but if we are going through life's difficulties, we learn patience and endurance.

Therefore, studying the Bible helps us grow in patience.
As the Holy Revelation says: "For all that has been written is written for our teaching, so that with patience and consolation in what is in the Scriptures we will have hope." (Rom 15:4)
, Satan can defeat a believer who does not know his Bible but he cannot defeat a believer who understands God's purposes in Scripture

3. The position of the will submitted to God

" Let your patience show itself perfectly .... " (James 1:4)
God uses temptations to wean us from the world.
God's purpose for our lives is to attain spiritual maturity.
The difficult stage is the pre-maturity stage, which is the stage of weaning.

David said, "I calmed down and kept quiet my soul like a weaner toward his mother, my soul towards you as a wean"

(Ps 131:2). But if we do not surrender to God, we will not benefit, and we may even stay longer in our spiritual childhood. In verses 9-11, the apostle James speaks of two types of believers: the poor and the rich. God deals with the poor and fills him with spiritual riches that rejoice in his heart, and the rich also rejoice in the riches of Christ that are so much spiritually.

When the test comes to the poor, he asks God to take his way and rejoice because he has spiritual riches that are never taken away from him. And when the test comes upon the rich, he also asks God to take his way and rejoice because he has riches in Christ that never ends and does not fade. Therefore, comfort does not come from the money in our hands, but from God's spiritual blessings.

4. The attitude of the heart open to faith

"If any of you lacks wisdom, let him seek God" (James 1:5). The apostle James writes to people who have problems with prayer. The apostle James responds to this by saying, "If any of you lacks wisdom, let him ask God," for wisdom helps to understand God's purpose in trials. The Apostle James has much to say about wisdom, for he also says:
"Whoever is wise and knowledgeable among you, let him see his deeds by behaving well in the meekness of wisdom. .... but the wisdom that is from above is first pure, then peaceful, considerate, submissive, filled with mercy and good fruits, without doubt and hypocrisy" (James 3:13-18).

How do we seek wisdom?

Answer is by faith, unbelief or suspicion are enemies of God. And the Apostle James resembles a doubter with the waves of the sea, rising once and falling again. And we are in a position of doubt when we have the unfixed or double thought, faith says yes and unbelief says no, and here comes doubt and suspicion. It is the doubt that made Peter drown as he walked on water, (Matt 14:30-31) Jesus said to him, "O you of little faith, why have you doubted?" For Peter began to sink when he took his eyes off Jesus.

He says, "Blessed is the man who endures temptation," meaning that he is rewarded in his walk with God here, and then with the crown of life at the second coming of Christ.

- We rejoice in trials because we love God, and He loves us and does not allow us to get any harm.
- And we have the understanding thought because we know that God loves us, and we have shared His divine truth, and we love Him too.
- And we surrender our will to him because we love Him, and wherever there is love, there is obedience and submission.
- And we have a heart open to faith because love and faith go together, we love God, so we trust in Him.

If we return to the subject of weaning, we say: a child who loves his mother and is sure that his mother loves him, he progresses and grows. And the believer who loves God knowing that God loves him, is not disturbed when God allows him to go through trial, because he is safe in God's love. God's purpose for us from trials is maturity, so let us be patient, and let patience have a perfect work in us.

Second: Processing trials
How do we treat the trials? (James 1:13-18)

A mature believer endures trials, sometimes temptations are with God's permission to test faith, or they are from Satan to try to bring us down.

So, what is the relationship between the two here?

Simply we say, if we are not paying attention, tests from the outside can turn into temptations from the inside.

When things get tough for us, we begin to complain about God, doubt God's love, and then resist His will. At this point, Satan volunteers to help by offering us the opportunity to escape and providing us with the way to get rid of problems, so, that Satan's attempt, becomes the temptation itself. To

prevail over temptations, there are three facts that we must keep in mind:
1. To consider God's judgment (James 1:13-16)
2. To consider the righteousness of God (James 1:17)
3. To consider the will of God (James 1:18)

1. To consider God's judgment:

Where does sin end? He says it "produces death." So do not blame God, because He is Holy and because He loves us. The apostle James laid down sin in four stages:

(1) Lust (James 1:14), and he says: "Everyone is tempted if he is attracted and deceived by his lust."
Lust means all kinds of desires in life, and these desires, are natural functions in life, there is nothing wrong with them unless they are misused, when we want to satisfy our desires away from God's will, we fall into distress.

(2) Deception (James 1:14), "Everyone is tempted if he is attracted and deceived." And "attracted and deceived", carries in its meaning the idea of the bait found in the trap or the hook. The temptation always carries with it a bait that attracts our natural desires, and this bait hides the truth, so we do not realize the trap.

(3) Disobedience or disobeying. He says: "Then lust, if conceived, gives birth to sin, and sin, if it is completed, produces death" (James 1:15). Lust is about the **emotions**, and deception is about the **mind**, and disobedience is about the **will**.
Lust becomes pregnant if it takes the bait, the mind and the will agree and acts, the result is sin, sin produces death, and we have entered the trap. The Christian life is a will and not a feeling, the more we can say no to Satan, the more the Lord owns and controls our life. "For God is the worker in you, ..." (Philippians,2:13).

(4) Death. And he says: "And sin, if completed it produces death" (James 1:15)

If we obey God's Word, this helps us not to give in to temptations and helps us to sanctify in us our desires and the desires of life, so that Satan does not have any chance to tempt us.

God does not want us to die in sin, He says: "do I have any pleasure in the death of the wicked? says the Lord, rather than that he should turn from his ways and live?" (Ezekiel 18: 23)

Satan aroused lust in Eve, in ancient times, saying: "God knows that the day you eat of it, your eyes will be opened, and you will be like God, knowing good and evil (Gen 3:5) It is as if the devil wants to say: Is obtaining knowledge wrong? Is eating food wrong? Scripture says, "And the woman saw that the tree was good to eat" (Gen 3:6). And here the lust moved in her, and she did what God forbade her to do. Satan is a deceiver, and he always tries to deceive the thought and the mind, and the bait he used with Eve is that the forbidden tree is good and delicious, and eating from it gives her knowledge and wisdom.

So Eve saw the bait, and forgot the warning of the Lord, who said: "But do not eat of the tree of the knowledge of good and evil, for the day you eat of it, you will die" (Gen 2:17) And here Eve disobeyed the command of God, when she took of the fruit of the tree and ate, and gave her man also with her, and he ate, for he also showed his disobedience to God. Thus, Adam and Eve experienced spiritual death, which is separation from God. Thus, sin entered through Adam into the whole human race, and death became upon all.

The Bible says, "As in Adam all die, so in Christ all will live" (1 Cor 15:22).

We should be aware that God's judgment says, "The wages of sin is death" (Rom 6:23).

2. To consider the righteousness of God:
The Bible says: "Every good gift and every perfect gift is from

above coming down from the Father of lights, who has no change or shadow of rotation" (James 1:17).

One of the devil's tricks is that he tries to convince us that our Heavenly Father does not love us or care for us.

When Jesus was tempted, he said, "If the Father really loves you, why are you hungry?" But the answer to this is that: because God is good, we do not need anyone else to meet our needs. But if we doubt His goodness, we will be attracted to what Satan offers us, that is, to the bait.

The Apostle James gave four facts about God's goodness:

(1) God gives good gifts

Everything good in this world comes from God, and the thing that does not come from God is not good, but if it comes from God, it must be good, even if we do not see the good at that time.

The thorn that was given to Paul in the flesh was from God, and it seemed a strange gift in its appearance, but it was a cause of blessing to Paul. He says, " I have pleaded to the Lord three times to take it away from me. .... and he said unto me, my grace is sufficient for you, for my power is made perfect in weakness" (2 Cor 12:7- 9)

(2) The way in which God gives is good

The value of a gift lies in the way it is given. If the gift is not based on love, it loses its value. But God's gift to us is a blessing because He gives us out of love, and out of the reality of divine generosity.

(3) God constantly gives

He says, "Coming down from above," it is not seasonal, but God always and continuously gives, even if we do not see His gifts. However, He continues to give, so how do we know that? The answer is: because the Word of God tells us so, and the Word of God is true.

(4) God does not change

The Bible says, "He has no change, no shadow of rotation." God does not change because He is Holy, good, and perfect. And when the light of the sun changes, it is because of the

rotation of the earth, because the sun is always luminous.
When shadows enter between us and the Heavenly Father, it is not He who caused those shadows, but us.
God does not change.
When difficulties and trials come upon us, we must not doubt God's love and goodness.

3. To Consider God's Will

He says, "He chose to give birth to us ...." (James 1:18).
And this new birth is through the Word of God. The Lord Jesus said, "He who is born of the flesh is flesh, and he who is born of the Spirit is spirit" (Jn 3:6).
The experience of the new birth helps us to triumph over temptations, for the new birth is from Jesus Christ, Jesus Christ is the victor in us, and this new life needs to be nourished by the word every day, so that we become stronger day by day. And the Holy Spirit, who used the "word of truth," gave us spiritual birth, He also uses the word of God to give us the spiritual strength we need.
Jesus says, "Man does not live by bread alone, but by every word that proceeds from the mouth of God" (Matthew 4:4).
The word "firstborn" is a meaningful expression for the people, as they used to offer the firstborn in ancient times, as an expression of their devotion to God and their obedience to Him. When we offer our souls to God, we express our devotion and obedience to Him.

Third: The dangers arising from self-deception: Do not deceive yourselves (James 1:19-27)
He says, "You deceive your souls" (James 1:23).
"His heart is deceived" (James 1:26)
If a believer sins because Satan deceives him, this is a dangerous thing, but even more dangerous is that the believer

deceives himself.

The Lord Jesus says: "Many will say to me in that day, Lord, Lord, have we not prophesied in your name, cast out demons in your name, and in your name made many powers? Then I will declare to them, I have never known you, depart from me, you who do unrighteousness" (Mt 7:22)

The sign of maturity appears when a man confronts himself faithfully, knows himself, and admits his deficiency. But he who thinks that he is not spiritually needy, is immature, and God's saying applies to him, "I intend to vomit you from my mouth, for you say I am rich, and I have been rich, and I need nothing" (Rev 3:16, 17).

The Apostle James says that we have three responsibilities towards the Word of God:

1. To receive the Word, "Receive therefore by the meekness of the planted Word, which is able to save your souls" (James 1:21).

2. To practice the Word and apply it in practice "Be doers of the word" (James 1:23).

3. To share the Word with others "The pure and perfect religion with God the Father is this, to look after the orphans and widows in their tribulation, and the preservation of man himself unspotted from the world" (James 1:27).

1. To accept the Word

"Receive therefore the meekness of the planted word, which is able to save your souls" (James 1:21).

The apostle James calls the Word of God the Planted Word, quoting from the parable of the Sower offered by the Lord Jesus. (Matthew 13:1-9, 18-23) The Word of God does not work in our lives unless we accept it, in the right way. Jesus said, "See what you hear" (Mk 4:24) He also said, "See how you hear" (Lk 8:18). But there are people of whom Christ says, "Sighted do not see, and hearers do not hear or understand" (Mt 13:13). Many people attend church and listen to Bible lessons, but they show neither growth nor maturity. To accept

the Word of God, we must obey these directives:
(1) "quick to listen"
He says: "Whoever has ears to hear, let him hear" (Mt 13:9) And he says: "Faith comes by hearing and the hearing is of The Word of God " (Rom 10:17) Just as a servant hastens when he hears his master's voice, and just as a mother hastens when she hears her child's cry, so a believer must be quick to hear what God wants to say to him.

(2) "Slow to speak"
The Bible says, "But he who restrains his lips is wise" (Prov 10:19). And because we have two ears and one mouth, it reminds us that we must hear more than we speak. Let us not argue with the Word of God, not publicly or even in our conscience.

(3) "Slow in anger"
He says, "For the wrath of man does not bring the righteousness of God" (James 1:20).

Peter was slow to listen, quick to speak, quick in anger, and thus he was about to kill the servant of the high priest with his sword. And the apostle James warns us not to be angry with the Word of God, because that is sin. The Word of God tells us about the truth that reveals our sins.

Anger is the opposite of the patience that God wants to cultivate in a believer to be mature (James 1:3, 4)

In v. 21 he speaks of the preparation of the heart: "Therefore cast away all impurity and abundance of evil and accept with the meekness of the planted word that is able to save your souls." It likens the heart to an orchard, which, if left or neglected, produces only weeds.

And the apostle James exhorts us to take off the weeds and prepare the soil for the "planted word of God." To prepare the soil of the heart, we must confess our sins before God, meditate on God's love and rich grace, and ask Him to prepare our hearts to obey His Word.

Finally, we need to be filled with "meekness" (Jas 1:21). And meekness is the opposite of the anger spoken of in (Jas

1:19, 20).

When we accept the Word of God with meekness, we do not argue with it but hide it in our hearts so that we do not sin against God.

The fruit of the Word in us is:

New life, Christian behavior, Christian morals, and service to others for the glory of God.

This fruit helps to:

Winning souls for Christ, growing in the holy life, forming spiritual character, and behaving in good works.

2. The second responsibility is to practice the Word and apply it in practice. "Be doers of the Word" (Jas 1:23).

We may mistakenly think that simply listening to God's Word helps us grow, but the truth is that it is not listening to the Word but acting on the Word that brings us blessing.

One said that many believers put signs in their scriptures, but their scriptures showed no sign in them.

In the preceding paragraph, the apostle James likened the word of God to the seed and said: "The planted word."

Here he likens the word to a mirror and says: "If anyone is a hearer of the word and not a worker, it is like a man looking at his face in the mirror" (Jas 1:23).

The mirror tests our look and appearance, and the word of God tests our lives and our behavior.

The Apostle James mentions some of the mistakes that people make when they look in the mirror of the Word of God:

(1) They look at it but do not meditate on it with care and interest and thus do not benefit from it personally.

This is because fleeting reading in the Bible does not meet the spiritual needs of man. Whoever wants to benefit from reading God's Word must act like a diver who descends into the depths in search of pearls and pearls.

(2) The second mistake is that they forget what they read. He says, "He looked at himself, and passed away, and for a time he forgot what it was" (Jas 1:24). If they had looked and read from the depth of their hearts, they would never have forgotten

what they had read.

(3) The third mistake is that they do not obey what the Word of God requires of them.

It is easier for believers to hear the Word than to do it, or it is easier for them to speak it and not to do it.

If we want to benefit from the mirror of God's Word, we must look at it carefully. We must test our hearts as well as our lives in the light of God's Word. This requires us to spend time, give attention, and dedicate devotion.

The true blessing comes from doing the word, not from hearing it. He says, "But whoever has become aware of the perfect law, the law of freedom, and abides and becomes not a forgetful hearer, but a worker of the word, this will be blessed in his work" (Jas 1:25).

James calls God's Word **"the perfect law of freedom,"** because if we obey Him, God sets us free.

For Christ said, "Whoever does sin is a slave to sin" (Jn 8:34). He also said, "If you abide in my words, you will indeed be my disciples, and you will know the truth, and the truth will set you free" (Jn 8:31, 32).

And if the mirror of the Word does the work of the test, it also helps us to return to God, and to regain our position with Him. For the Word also cleanses us. The Lord Jesus says, "You are now pure because of the words which I have spoken to you" (Jn 15:3).

And the Church is sanctified and purified "by washing the water with the word" (Eph 5:26). Reading the Word not only tests us but also helps us to wash away the filth of the world that may attach to us, and the blood of Christ "cleanses us from all sin."

And the third service of the Word mirror is that it changes our shape. God wants us to change so that we can overcome sin and self in us. He says, "As we all look upon the glory of the Lord with an unveiled face, as in a mirror, we are transformed into that same image, from glory to glory, as from the Lord the Spirit" (2 Cor 3:18).

This means that when a believer looks at the Word of God, which is like a mirror, he sees Jesus Christ, and then he is transformed by the Spirit of God so that he may have a share and have fellowship in the glory of God.

The word "change" in the original language means a change from the inside that appears on the outside.

The more time we spend diving into the Word of God where we see Jesus Christ in it, the more we change into the image of His glory within us, this appears in our daily lives. It is the same word with which the Holy Revelation described Jesus Christ while he was on the Mount of Transfiguration, saying: "And his form was changed before them, and his face shone like the sun" (Mt 17:2).

The same word is also found in (Rom 12:2), where it says, "... change your form by renewing your minds."

The important thing is to lift the veil, he says, "Not as Moses used to put a veil on his face, but when he returns to the Lord, he lifts up the veil" (2 Cor 3:13-16).

In front of the mirror of the Word, we say with the psalmist: "Test me, O God, and know my heart, test me and know my thoughts, and see if it is in a vain way, and guide me to an eternal way" (Ps 139:23, 24).

The first responsibility is to accept the word.

The second responsibility is to practice the word and apply it in our lives.

3 And the third responsibility is to share the Word with others. He says, "The pure and perfect religion of God the Father is this, to care for orphans and widows in their tribulation, and the preservation of man himself unstained from the world" (Jas 1:27).

Sharing with others: talking, serving, and isolating from the world. The saying: "If any of you thinks that he is a religious and he does not restrain his tongue but deceives his heart, then the religion of this is false" (Jas 1:26). The tongue reveals the heart, and if the heart is straight, the conversation is also straight.

Ministry: "The pure and perfect religion is the care of orphans and widows" (Jas 1:27). We have seen our souls in the mirror of the Word, and we have seen Christ, so we must see the needs of others as well. Isolation from the world: "... And man preserved himself pure and unstained from the world" (Jas 1:27)

The world is placed in the evil one, and his ruler is Satan. And we need to be careful not to conform to this world, but to change our form, so that we may retain our strong witness in Christ. We must keep ourselves isolated from the world so that we can serve others.

Chapter Two

The rich and the poor (James 2: 1-13)

1 The divinity of Christ

"My brethren and sisters' believers in our Lord Jesus Christ, Lord of glory, you must not have favoritism" (Jas 2:1).
Jesus Christ is Lord of glory (Jas 2:1- 4)
Jesus did not favor faces, and his enemies also knew this about him, and they said, "Teacher, we know that you are true, and you know the way of God in truth and do not care about anyone, for you do not look at the faces of men" (Mt 22:16). Jesus looked at the heart and was not moved by the rich or by the social status, and the widow who threw two pennies

into the treasury was in his eyes greater than the rich Pharisees. Jesus warned the religious leaders, saying, "Do not judge according to what is apparent, ..." (Jn 7:24). We tend to judge people by their appearance, so we do not like to sit with some people because they are not our type. But Jesus was a friend of sinners, though He did not approve of their sins. He forbade religious leaders to judge according to appearance. He said, "Judge not according to appearance, but judge justly" (Jn 7:24).
How do we practice the faith of our Lord Jesus Christ, Lord of Glory, in our dealings with others?
We must look at each one through Christ, and if he is a Christian, we accept him, because Christ lives in him. And if he is not a Christian, we accept him because Jesus died for him or her. Christ is the link between us and others.

2. God's grace:

"Has God not chosen the poor of this world to be rich in faith" (Jas 2:5)

The emphasis here is on "choice". And the choice is made based on the grace of God. If our salvation were based on our merit, it would not have been by grace, and we would never be saved, because we are not worthy.

But God saved us, and still is saving, because of Christ's work on the cross. He says, "By grace you are saved" (Eph 2:5).

God does not look at differences and does not care about differences. Masters and slaves, poor and rich, all are equal to Him. And the apostle James teaches us that the grace of God makes the poor rich, because he inherits the riches of grace in Christ. He says, "Listen, my beloved brethren, has God not chosen the poor of this world, rich in faith, and heirs of the kingdom that He promised it to those who love Him" (Jas 2:5)

But the rich man who relies on his wealth will benefit nothing. Man can be poor in this world, rich in eternity, or rich in this world, but poor in eternity.

The Bible says: "I command the rich in this present age not to be arrogant, nor to cast their hope on the uncertainty of riches, but on the living God" (2 Tim 6:17). And man can be poor here, poor in eternity, and he can be rich here, and rich in eternity.

He says: "I command the rich in the present age..., to do good, and to be rich in good works, to save for themselves a good foundation for the future, so that they may hold eternal life" (2 Tim 6:17-19).

God has promised the kingdom to those who love Him, not to those who love the world. (Jas 2:5)

"But you have humiliated the poor, and is it not the rich who rule over you while they drag you to the courts? Are they not blaspheming the good name? (Jas 2:6, 7)

And he wants to say that they despise the poor, and act like the rich who are not saved by the grace of Christ.

In those days, the rich were exploiting the poor, and they were using their influence to get court rulings against them, and they were getting richer at the expense of the poor.

Unfortunately, nowadays we find believers doing the same thing, committing the same sins, and bringing shame on the name of Christ. God's grace teaches us to deal with others based on God's plan, not based on human merit or social status.

When Jesus died on the cross, he broke down the middle wall of the Temple that separated the Jews from the Gentiles.

At his birth, he was born in a despicable manger, and he broke down the barrier between the rich and the poor, between the young and the old, and between the educated and the uneducated, and it is wrong to rise and build this wall again.

3. The Word of God

"If ye fulfill the royal law according to the Scriptures, thou shalt love thy neighbor as thyself, ye shall do well" (Jas 2:8). James returned to the Old Testament to present us with one of God's commandments: "Love your neighbor as yourself." (Leviticus 19:18)

In the parable of the Good Samaritan, Jesus told us that it is the neighbor who needs help. (Lk 10:25-37).

The important question here is not: Who is my relative? It is: who can I be close to?

He says, "If you fulfill the royal law, why is the commandment to "love your neighbor as yourself" considered to be the royal law?

The answer is:

(1) For it was given by the king, for God the Father gave it in the law, and God the Son fixed it to his disciples (Jn 13:34) and God the Holy Spirit fills our hearts with the love of God and expects us to share it with others. (Rom 5:5)

Hatred makes a man a slave, but love makes him a master. Love helps us to obey the Word of God, and to treat others as God commands us.

(2) Because it surpasses all commandments, for love is the fulfillment of the law. (Rom 13:10)

If every man loved his brother, there would be no need for many complex laws.

Love does not mean that I am committed to agreeing with all people in everything, but Christian love is to treat others the same way God treats me.

Love is the work of the will and not the work of passion, and the motivation is to glorify God.

4. The Divine Decree:

"... Judge by the law of freedom" (Jas 2:21)

As Christians, we are not judged for our sins because they have been forgiven in the blood of Christ, who has become the atonement for our sins, and He is also the intercessor. But we will be judged for our words. He says, "... And you looked at the one who was clothed in the splendid garment and said to him, 'Sit here you are well,' and you said to the poor man, 'Stand there or sit here under my footstool, have you not discriminated among yourselves and become judges with evil thoughts?'" (Jas 2:3).

For we will give an account of every idle word that we speak (Matthew 12:36)

And the Lord Jesus says, "Out of the virtue of the heart speaks the mouth" (Mt 12:34) and we will be judged for our deeds.

The apostle Paul says: "We must all appear before the seat of Christ, so that everyone may receive what was in the flesh according to what he has done, good or evil" (2 Cor 5:10).

The promise is true that God no longer mentions our sins, as in (Jer. 31:34) and (Heb 10:17).

But what about the bad results of our bad deeds? God forgives us our sins when we confess them before Him, but it does not change the consequences of it, so He says, "But when we have been judged, we are disciplined by the Lord, that we may not be judged with the world" (1 Cor 11:32). We will be judged for our positions. "For judgment is without mercy to him who does not do mercy, and mercy boasts of judgment" (Jas 2:13). If we show mercy towards others, God shows mercy towards us. Mercy and justice are both from God, and there is no competition between them. When there is repentance and there is faith, God has mercy. But with rebellion and unbelief, God judges justly.

Why does the apostle James use this expression: "the law of freedom"?

(1) For when we obey the law of God, He frees us from sin and helps us walk in freedom.

(2) Because it equips us for freedom, we have given the commandment by the law that we may be trained to obey the commandment without the law. Let us be free from the law and walk freely in Christ.

(3) For the Word of God changes us and makes us willing to do the will of God, so that we obey from within our hearts by our will, not from outside by command and prohibition, and with that we will reach the spiritual maturity.

Incorrect faith
(James 2:14- 26)

The key to the Christian life is faith, for the sinner is saved by faith (Eph 2:8, 9), the believer must walk by faith (2 Cor 5:7), without faith is unpleasing to God (Heb 11:6), and everything that is not of faith is sin, as in (Rom 14:23).

One of them said in the definition of faith: The right faith is to obey God no matter what the results. And when we read Heb 11, which is the chapter of faith, we find men and women who walked according to the Word of God, whatever the cost.

Faith is the confidence that God's Word is true, and that acting according to God's Word brings God's blessing.

Here the Apostle James examines the relationship between faith and works and tells us here that there are three types of faith, and only one of them is true faith:

1. Dead faith
2. The Faith of Demons
3. Active faith, and this is the right faith.

1. Dead faith

He says: "If a brother and sister are naked and destitute for daily sustenance, one of you says to them, 'Go in peace, be warm and satisfied.' But you did not give them the needs of the body, so what is the benefit? (Jas 2:15)

Some people give words instead of deeds, and they think that speech takes the place of deeds, and this is not true. So how can it be that talking helps the needy to relieve his needs? As Christians, we have an obligation to participate in addressing the needs of people, whether they are sincere or unfaithful. The Bible says, "As we have an opportunity, let us do good for all, especially for the people of faith" (Gal 6:10).

Helping a person in need is an expression of love, and we know that faith works with love, as in (Gal 5:6). The apostle James attaches special importance to this thought about good works, so the question here is in Jas 2:14: "Can faith save him?" That is, this faith that does not work with love.

The answer is: No, this kind of faith is dead. In Jas 2:17 it says: "So is faith also, if it does not have works, it is dead in itself".

The theologian Kelvin said: Only faith can save, but faith that saves does not remain alone, without works.

The one who has dead faith, has only a knowledge experience, he knows the teaching of salvation, but he did not submit himself to God, and he did not believe in Christ for salvation. He knows the right words, but he does not support them by works.

The apostle James warns against the faith without works, that it is dead, three times in verses (17, 20, 26).

2. Faith of demons:

"... And the demons believe and shudder" (Jas 2:19)

Man is shocked at first sight when he knows that demons have faith, so what is their faith? They believe in the existence of God; they are neither atheists nor believers. They also believe in the divinity of Christ, and they bear witness that Christ is the Son of God (Mk 3:11, 12), they believe there is a place of punishment (Lk 8:31), and they also know Jesus Christ as The Judge (Mk 5:1-13), and subject to the authority of his word.

He says, "You believe that God is one, 0 Well you do, and the demons believe and shudder" (Jas 2:19).

And the apostle James says that the right faith that saves can be seen, and so the new life can be seen.

He says, "Show me your faith without works, and I will show you my faith by my works" (Jas 2:18).

How can a dead sinner do works of love, or works of faith? Impossible.

But when we believed in Christ, we became a new creation in Him. He says, "We were created in Christ Jesus for good works God has prepared it for us to walk in it" (Eph 2:10).

3. Active faith:
And this is the faith that saves.
He says, "So Abraham believed in God, and righteousness was given to him" (Jas 2:23).

Effective faith is the right faith that saves, and it is the one that changes life for the better. And this working faith is based on the Word of God (Jas 1:18) And the Word of God saves us if we accept it (Jas 1:21)

He says: "Faith comes by hearing and the hearing through the word of God" (Rom 10:17)

James cites two explanations of active faith that is saved, and he introduces Abraham and Rahab to us, because both have heard God's message and accepted it.

Abraham was a Jew, but Rahab was a Gentile. Abraham was a pious man, but Rahab was a sinful and fallen woman. Abraham was the friend of God, but Rahab followed enemies of God. So, what brought them together?

The answer is: Both experienced salvation by faith.

The Bible says of Abraham that he was justified by faith, (Rom 4), whose life has been justified and changed, and he obeys God's will. And his faith is manifested in his works.

James uses an incident in Abraham's life, namely the presentation of his son Isaac on the altar (Gen 22), this confirms that he is justified by faith, and his faith is manifested in his obedience to God.

This does not mean that Abraham is justified by faith and works, but by faith that does works.

And the second clarification is about Rahab, the story is written in (Josh 2) and in (Josh 6). The story goes that Joshua sent spies to the Promised Land before they entered it, and the spies met Rahab the harlot, which provided them with refuge, and protected them until they departed. She confessed that she believed in God's words, and the men promised her that they would keep her and her family when they returned and entered the city. We should test ourselves, are we in faith? And we say with the psalmist: "Test me, O God, and know my heart, test me and know my thoughts, and see if it is in a vain way, and guide me to an everlasting way" (Ps 139:23, 24)

Chapter Three
Tongue control
(James 3:1-12)

In the first chapter, the Apostle James showed us one of the characteristics of a mature believer, which is that:
    1. Patient in distress
The second characteristic is mentioned in the second chapter, which is that:
    2. Living the Christian life in practice
In chapter three, he tells us that the third characteristic of a mature believer is that:
    3. Tongue control
It appears that the believers to whom the Apostle James writes, have serious problems resulting from the lack of control of the tongue. He advised them to be quick to listen, slow to speak, slow in anger (Jas 1:19).

He says: "If no man restrained his tongue but deceives his heart, the religion of this is false" (Jas 1:26).

We are to speak and act as if we are facing Jesus Christ at the trial. He says, "So speak and so do it, as you are to be judged by the law of freedom" (Jas 2:12) God has given us the blessing of using the tongue in good talking. We praise

God with the tongue, pray with the tongue, preach with the tongue, and lead people to Christ with the tongue, what a great Privilege.

But with this same tongue we can lie in a way that discredits others or breaks the heart of an innocent human being. Here are six pictures of the tongue:

The bridle – the rudder – the fire - a monster or a poisonous animal - a fountain - a fig tree

We can put the six images in three meanings that express the strength of the tongue:

1. Power that manages
2. Power that destroys
3. Power that delights

1. Power that manages:

The rudder - bridle (Jas 3:1- 4) He says, "If anyone does not stumble in speech, that is a perfect man who is able to restrain the whole body also" (Jas 3:2). Behold, the ships are also so great and driven by gusty winds that turn them by a very small rudder wherever he wills." (Jas 3:4)

It appears that everyone in the church wanted to teach and be a spiritual leader, so that the apostle James says to them: "Do not be many teachers, my brethren, ... " (Jas 3:1) He who knows must use the tongue to share with others the divine truth, and at the same time he must live what he speaks, otherwise his teaching is hypocrisy.

But sin is not limited to teachers, for it says in Jas 3:2, "For in many things we all stumble." A man who can control his tongue proves that he can control the whole body as a mature human being. The bridle and rudder are small, but they do an excellent job, just like the tongue in the flesh. A small bridle helps the horse rider to control it completely, and a small rudder helps the captain of a large ship to control it and lead it.

The tongue is a small organ in the body, but it has a great

power to do dangerous things, and we have the old nature which wants to control and wants to make us make mistakes, and sometimes we are found in circumstances that make us say words that we should not speak. This means that the bridle and rudder must be in strong and controlling hands.

The Bible warns, "Death and life are in the hands of the tongue" (Prov 18:21). No wonder that David prayed saying "Lord, make a guardian of my mouth. Guard the door of my lips" (Ps 141)

And the Lord Jesus says, "Out of the bounty of the heart speaks the mouth" (Mt 12:34). When the Lord Jesus Christ controls the heart, He also controls the lips.

2. Power that destroys:

Fire - Beast (Jas 3:5- 8) He says: "Behold, there is little fire, a fuel that burns, and the tongue is fire, ... " (Jas 3:6).

For every character of beasts and birds, skies, and sea is humiliated, and it may be under control to the human nature. But the tongue no one of the people can control it" (Jas 3:7, 8)

If you do not resist the little spark, it gets bigger and most of the fire is from the smallest spark.

And we hear and read about fires that burned in houses and destroyed them, and people who were burned in them, and the losses of materials and loss of life are significant.

Our words can ignite a fire. And like fire, the tongue can raise the temperature of things.

"I said I will watch my ways and keep and keep my tongue from sin, I will put a muzzle on my mouth while in the presence of the wicked" (Ps 39:1-3)

And fire is also defiled, for the waste it leaves behind, with the smell of combustion and the distortion it causes, is considered an impurity that needs restoration, decoration, and beautification.

Words of fire can defile the house, the church, and society. And nothing can wash away this filth except the blood of Jesus

Christ.

Jesus suffered in the days of his flesh on earth, because of the words described by his enemies. They have said that He eats and drinks wine (Matthew 11:19) And when He had performed miracles, they said of Him that He was in agreement with Satan, and that He cast out demons by beelzebub. Even when He was on the cross, they hurt Him with their words

"The tongue is the fire of the world of iniquity. Thus, has been placed in our members the tongue that defiles the whole body, and burns the circle of the universe, and burns from hell" (Jas 3:6)

Fire destroys, and the tongue also destroys. The words we utter have the power of destruction. It can break hearts and reputed people and destroy souls and sent them to eternity without Christ.

Therefore, we must make our conversation full of grace, and repaired with salt (Cor 4:6)

The tongue is also like a beast. Not only is the tongue like fire, but it is also like a predatory beast, and it is restless and cannot be controlled. Some animals are poisonous, and the tongue is sometimes poisonous. And the trick about poison is that it works secretly and slowly, but it finally kills.

Do they release hungry beasts or poisonous snakes among people? Of course not, but the tongue can do its job and achieves the same results as it. And the apostle James says that beasts may humble themselves to the human nature, and fire also can be controlled, except the tongue, no one can control it. And the heart is the foundation, and if the heart is filled with hatred, the devil lights the fire. But if the heart is filled with love, then God He is the one who ignites the fire, the fire of the Holy Spirit.

3. Power that delights:

The Spring - the Figs (Jas 3:9-12)

"Is there a fountain that springs from the same fountain sweet and bitter? Can a fig tree, my brothers, make olives? or can a vine make figs? Or likewise a fountain that makes water that is fresh and salty?" (Jas 3:11, 12).

The spring springs water for us, and we need water in our daily lives, water is life for man, and our words also can give life, and water if not controlled, causes destruction, so does the tongue. When floods rise, they sink and destroy, so does the tongue. The Bible says: "Death and life are in the hands of the tongue" (Prov 18:21).

Water also purifies, and the Word of God is spiritual water that cleanses us (Jn 15:3).

And the tongue is also a force that delights, for it is like a tree that brings joy and makes lush shadows as it bears fruit. Our words can help the helpless to find comfort and shelter, and the tired traveler to find encouragement. The Bible says: "The lips of the righteous guide many" (Proverbs 10:21). That is, we can satisfy a hungry soul in righteousness and peace. And the Lord Jesus said, "The words which I speak to you are spirit and life" (Jn 6:63).

The important thing for the tree is the root. If the root does not extend deep into the soil, the tree does not grow well.
He says: "Like a tree planted at the streams of water, which bears fruit in its time, and its leaves do not wither" (Ps 1:3). "The Lord has given me the tongue of the educated, that I may know how to help the weary by a word" (Is 50:4)

How much we need to meet the Lord every day, talk to Him to learn from Him, and we need to deepen the spiritual roots in His Word. And the apostle James says that the fountain does not spring from the same fountain fresh water and bitter water. And one tree does not give two different types of fruit. The tongue with which "we bless God the Father and with which we curse men" is in dire need of the transformative work of God's grace. He says, "Out of one mouth comes a blessing and a curse. It is not fit, brethren, that these things should be like this" (Jas 3:10).

True wisdom and false wisdom
(James 3: 13- 18)

"He who is wise and scholar among you, let him do his deeds by behaving well in the meekness of wisdom" (Jas 3:13).

Meekness is not weakness, but disciplined strength, and it is also a fruit of the Holy Spirit. (Gal 5:23)

We need to apply God's commandments and words to our lives every day, but when we cannot connect the essence of the message, in our spiritual and daily life, our knowledge is without wisdom, it is not enough to have knowledge only, because we need wisdom so that we can use knowledge correctly. Therefore, the Apostle James warns those who want to be teachers in the Church, abstract knowledge makes us separate and divide, but wisdom helps us to gather and unite, and to benefit from divine truth in our daily lives.

Here we find a contrast between true wisdom and false wisdom in three aspects:

1. Interview in the source (Jas 3:15-17)

True wisdom comes from above, but false wisdom comes from below. In other words, there is heavenly wisdom that comes from God, and there is human wisdom that does not come from God, but rather from human.

What is the source of human wisdom?

He says, "This wisdom is not coming down from above, but it is a satanic psychological earthly." (Jas 3:15).

The believer has three enemies: the world, the flesh, and the devil (Eph 2:1-3) These three enemies are matched by descriptions of human wisdom.

The Bible says: "The beginning of wisdom is the fear of the Lord and the knowledge of the Holy One, is understanding"

(Prov 9:10). The world in its wisdom did not know God and rejected the gospel of Christ.

The Bible says: "The word of the cross to those who are perishing is foolishness" (1 Cor 1:18). This wisdom is psychological, i.e., natural (from nature). The original word means life or soul, and in (1 Cor 2:14) the word is translated (natural), that is, the opposite of spiritual, where He says: "But the natural man does not accept what belongs to the Spirit of God, because he has ignorance." And in Jude 19 it is translated (psychological).

He says, "... psychics, they don't have the spirit." This wisdom is satanic and this is shown in the serpent's success in deceiving Eve and so over time the wisdom of Satan fights against the wisdom of God, and Satan, who is the old serpent, is cunning, and was able to convince Eve that she would be like God, and that the tree will make her wise. If we do not know the wisdom of God, Satan can deceive us with his wisdom. And by contrast between this wisdom, which is Satanic psychological earthly, the apostle James describes the wisdom that comes from above in (Jas 1:17): every good gift and every perfect gift is from above coming down from the Father of lights."

Yes, the believer lifts his eyes up in all that he needs, his homeland is in heaven (Philippians 3:20), and his father is in heaven, (Matthew 6:16), and he is born from above (Jn 3:3), and his hope is in heaven as he seeks what is above (Cor 3:1). The believer finds that the source of true wisdom is God. He says, "If any of you lacks wisdom, let him seek God" (Jas 1:5).

And Jesus Christ became wisdom for us (1 Cor 1:30). The Bible also says of Jesus Christ: "He has all the treasures of wisdom and knowledge in him" (Cor 2:3).

2. Interview in performance (Jas 3:13, 14, 17)

God's wisdom works differently from earthly, psychological, satanic wisdom.

What is the evidence for false wisdom?
-Jealousy:
It means ambition and selfish enthusiasm.
Is our enthusiasm for the Lord spiritual or physical? And our jealousy for the Lord, spiritual or physical? Do we rejoice for the success of others, or do we envy them and criticize them? Do we help others when they fail, or do we be happy about it and leave them?
-Partisanship:
It means that man seeks to win as many people as possible to his side, and this creates competitors and opponents. But the Bible teaches us something different, saying, "We think of one thing, nothing by partisanship or wonder, but by humility and humbly" (Philippians 2:3)
-Pride:
Pride is always boasting, and human wisdom loves boasting. But when God's wisdom is at work, there will be no room for boasting, but humility, submission, and seeking the glory of God.
-Cheating:
He says: "... Do not boast and lie about the truth" (Jas 3:14). Selfish ambition leads to partisanship and competition, and for a person to win the round, he needs to boast, and boasting is a habit that includes lying, cheating and deception. But the wisdom that comes down from above, it is:
-Pure:
This refers to holiness. God is Holy, so the wisdom that comes down from above is pure. God's wisdom leads to the purity of life, but human wisdom leads to sin.
-Peaceful:
Human wisdom leads to competition and war, as he says: "Where are wars and rivalries between you from? Here, from your desires that battle within you? (James 4:1,2) But God's wisdom leads to peace, peace that is based on holiness.
-Gentle:

A companion person does not cause fighting, but he does not compromise on the truth to keep the peace.

-Acquiescent:
The wisdom that comes down from God makes the believer obedient to God, responsive and easy to share. But the earthly wisdom it makes man is difficult and stubborn, so a person who responds does not tolerate what he believes.

-Full of mercy:
The word "full" means under the control or under the rule of. He who follows the wisdom of God, is under the control of mercy. Jesus said, "Be merciful, as your Father is also merciful" (Lk 6:36). And the story of the Good Samaritan expresses mercy. The strange Samaritan, who took care of the wounded Jew, did not reap the reward, something material from behind his work, but he obeyed God and did his will, and the wounded man could not repay him anything for his work, and this is mercy.

-Good fruits:
Faithful people are fruitful. The wisdom of God does not make life empty, but makes it full and bears fruit, and The Holy Spirit brings fruits in the believer for the glory of God.

-Unsuspecting:
The wisdom of the world does not make us abide by one thought, so we fall into doubt. But the wisdom of God does not make man doubts, for the wisdom coming down from above brings strength.

-Without hypocrisy:
And the original word for hypocrisy means the one who wears the mask, when there is God's wisdom, there is honesty and there is truthfulness

3. Interview in results (Jas 3:16-18)
Worldly wisdom produces worldly results, while spiritual wisdom produces spiritual results. Worldly wisdom produces jealousy, partisanship, confusion, and every bad thing (Jas

3:16)
And it seems that God is not at work in that community where these things exist. The important thing is to measure our lives and our ministry on the Word of God, not according to human wisdom.

The battles and wars that exist between believers, the division of the churches, the lack of purity and the loss of peace, all this indicates the existence of a mistake ... and that is the loss of wisdom coming down from above. But God's wisdom produces a blessing.

He says, "And the fruit of righteousness shall be sown in peace by those who make peace" (Jas 3:18).

The word "fruit" means the results of life, and the fruit usually has seeds, and the seeds produce more fruit.

Whenever we share the fruit with others, the fruit produces fruit, and so on.

He says, "And the fruit of righteousness shall be sown in peace." The believer who obeys the wisdom of God sows' righteousness not sin and peace not war. The life of a believer is a life of sow and harvest. If we live in the wisdom of God, we sow righteousness and peace and reap the blessing of God. "a man reaps what he sows" (Gal 6:7)

And finally: "Blessed is the man who finds wisdom, ... " (Proverbs 3:13).

Chapter Four

How to end wars
(James 4:1-12)

"Where are the wars and rivalries between you?" (Jas 4:1) In this passage, the Apostle James talks about wars, says that there are three wars that exist, and he also tells us how we can end these wars.

1. War with our selves (Jas 4:1-3)

He says: "Where are the wars and rivalries between you, is it not from your desires that battle within you?" (Jas 4:1)

War within the heart helps war everywhere, in the home, in the church and in society. "If there is bitter jealousy and partisanship in your hearts" (Jas 3:14,16) Selfish desires are very dangerous, and they lead to wrong behaviors: "You desire, you kill, you envy." If our requests and prayers were wrong, our lives as believers are all wrong.

The commandment says, "Do not covet," and breaking it causes a break of all other commandments. Lust can make the person kill, and speaking lies, and not honoring his father and mother, and committing adultery, and breaking all the law of God. Those who Lust are unhappy in their lives, because instead of thanking God for what He has given them, they grumble because of what they do not have and always envy others and always ask for a magical work that changes their lives, while the real problem is within their hearts.

2. War with God (Jas 4:4-10)

He says: "Do you not know that loving the world is enmity towards God?" (James 4:4)

The root cause of every war, whether internal or external, is rebellion against God, i.e., disobedience. "Whoever commits sin does transgression, and sin is transgression" (1 Jn 3:4) How can a believer declare war on God?

A believer can declare war on God by befriending God's enemies, namely: the world, the body, and the devil.

(1) The world:

"Do you not know that loving the world is enmity against God? (James 4:4) Friendship with a community that is far from God, causes defilement from the world. In (Jas 1:27) the Apostle James speaks on "Man has kept himself immaculate from the world." And this friendship leads to the love of the world, while the Bible teaches us not to love the world.

He says, "Do not love the world, nor the things that are in the world" (1 Jn 2:15). This is because our love for the world makes it easy for us to conform to the world, and the Bible says: "Do not be like this age, but change from your form ..." (Rom 12:2)

The believer's endorsement of the world is considered a betrayal of God and is compared to adultery. The believer became connected with Christ, a connection like marriage (Rom 7:4), and he should be faithful to Christ.

The world is an enemy of God, and anyone who wants to be a friend of the world cannot be a friend of God.

(2) The second enemy is the flesh (Jas 4:1-5)

And the body in the sense of the old nature that we inherited from Adam. The Holy Spirit can use the flesh to glorify God, or the old nature can use the flesh to serve sin. But when the sinner surrenders to Christ, he takes a new nature within himself. For the old nature desires against the new nature, he says, "For the flesh desires against the spirit, and the spirit against and these two resist one another, until you do what you do not want" (Gal 5:17) This is what the apostle James means when he says, "Yourself is fighting in your members" (Jas 4:1).

So, to live in the flesh, it grieves the Spirit of God who lives in us. He says, "Or do you think that the Scripture says in vain, the Spirit that dwells in us longs for envy" (Jas 4:5)?
Yes, the Spirit who is in us guards us with the utmost jealousy in order to maintain our relationship with God.

So, The Holy Spirit grieves in us when we sin against God's love. To live to satisfy the old nature means that we are declaring war on God. The mind governed by the flesh is enmity against God" (Rom 8:7)

He also says, "For the concern of the flesh is death, but the concern of the Spirit is life and peace" (Rom 8:6).

(3) The third enemy is Satan (Jas 4:6, 7)

The world is in conflict with the Father, the flesh fights against the Holy Spirit, and Satan resists the Son of God.
Pride is Satan's great sin, and it is one of the dangerous weapons he uses against the saints. God wants us to be humble, Satan wants us to be proud. God wants us to rely on His grace, while Satan wants us to depend on our souls.
How can we be friends of God and not love the world?
The Apostle James gives us three directions for this:

(1) "Submit to God" (Jas 4:7)

That is to say, to surrender all to Him, and if there are things in our lives that are not given to God, this causes war, not peace.

He says, "Resist the devil, and he will flee from you" (Jas 4:7). The way to resist Satan is to submit to God.

(2) "Draw near to God" (Jas 4:8)

How do we draw near to God? That is by confessing our sins, asking for forgiveness and purification. He says, "Purify your hands, you sinners, and purify your hearts, you double minded." (Jas 4:8). And this is like spiritual adultery (James 4:4). The closer we get to God, the more we change to His image.

(3) "Humble yourselves before the Lord" (Jas 4:10)
We can be subdued by outward appearance yet not be humble before the Lord from within. God hates pride as in (Proverbs 6:16, 17), he disciplines the proud believer until he humbles himself.

Our position as believers towards God's will (James 4:13-17)

The Apostle James gives us three pictures of the attitude of believers towards God's will, and only one of them is correct:
    1- Ignoring God's Will
    2- Disobeying God's Will
    3- Obedience to God's will and this is the right attitude.

1- Ignoring God's will
"Come now, you who say, 'We will go today or tomorrow,' instead of saying, 'If the Lord wills and we live, we will do this or that.' (James 4:13-15)

The Apostle James seems to be addressing the rich merchants of the church, and they may have been proud of their plans that they were laying out, there is no evidence that they were seeking God's will, or that they were praying for their trade. But they measured their success in life by how many times they succeeded in accomplishing what they had planned for themselves, and how many times they gained from their pursuit of their trade.

The apostle James presented four truths that reveal their stupidity in ignoring God's will:

(1) Life is complicated (Jas 4:13)
Life is complicated by thinking about today and tomorrow, buying and selling, gaining, and losing, going to here and there, to this city or to that. Life has become the industry of

people, places and activities, goals, days, and years. Day after day away from God's will. That is why life is mysterious and complicated. But when we recognize Jesus Christ as our personal Savior, and do His will with all our hearts, then our life has meaning.

(2) Life without certainty, and no confirmation in it. He says, "You who do not know the matter of tomorrow" (Jas 4:14) Those merchants or businessmen were making plans for an entire year, even though they could not see what it was coming upon them in one day.

"Today or tomorrow, we go to this or that city and there we spend one year and trade and profit."

This reminds us of the stupid rich man with whom Jesus set an example in (Lk 12:16-21), he said: "I will destroy my stores and build the greatest, and I gather there all my yields and goods and I say to myself, O soul, you have many goods laid down for many years, rest and eat and drink and rejoice". God said to him, you fool, tonight your soul is asked from you. So, this is what you have prepared will be for whom?

Life is uncertain for us, but when we are in God's will, we have confidence in tomorrow's command, because we know that God is the one who guides us.

(3) Life is short:

"For what is your life? It is a vapor that appears a little and then disappear" (Jas 4:14) Life for us is long, and we measure it in years, but compared to eternity, it is like steam. Job said, "My days are swifter than a weaver's shuttle, and they come to an end without hope" (Job 7:6).

He also said, "Man is born of a woman with few days and full of trouble" (Job 14:1).

And because life is so short, it is better to invest it for eternal life, so we must put God's will first.

He says, "Instead of saying, 'If the Lord wills and we live,' (Jas 4:15)

How do we know God's will?
God reveals to us and reveals His will in His Holy Word. The Word of God teaches us the will of God. And knowing and studying it is the sure way to success.

He says: "The book of this law shall not depart from your mouth, but you shall meditate in it day and night, that you may be reserved to act according to all that is written in it, for then thou shalt fix thy way, and then thou shalt prosper" (Joshua 1:8).

(4) Bad pride:
"But now you boast in your magnification. Every boast like this is bad" (Jas 4:16)

Man boasts to cover his weakness, and he cannot judge the events to come. He cannot see the future, and he has no power to control the future. So, when a man boasts of this matter, he commits sin, for by doing so he puts himself in the position of God. He who ignores God's will is like a man who goes out into a forest and does not have a map to show him the roads, or to a journey in a rough sea and a stormy wind, and he does not have a compass to guide him on the way.

2- Disobeying God's Will:
"Whoever knows how to do well and not to do it, it is a sin for him" (Jas 4:17).

These people know God's will, but they have chosen for themselves not to obey it, because of the sin of pride. Pride man boasts that he is the master of his destiny, and that he is the leader of his life. And because he has accomplished wondrous and amazing things, so he thinks that he can do everything, as if he wants to say to God, "I know what you want me to do, but I don't want to.

Thus, it is fulfilled in them to say: "for it would have been better for them if they had not known the way of righteousness, than for after they had known they would turn away from the Holy Commandment" (2 Pet 2:21)

Man disobeys God's will because he is ignorant of its nature. God's will is not a recipe or a combination for an unhappy life, on the contrary, it is disobedience to God's will that leads to miserable life. Likewise, it is not an optional command, whether we accept it or reject it, but God's will is an obligation that the believer must accept. Because He is The Creator and we are His creation, and He is the Lord, the Master, and the Savior, and we are His children and His servants, so we must obey Him.

What happens to believers who disobey God's will?

They are disciplined by God until they are submitted. He says, "If you tolerate discipline, God will treat you like sons. But if you are without chastisement, in which all have become participating, then you are not sons" (Heb 12:5-11)

There is also the risk of losing reward, and the apostle Paul compares the believer to the athlete who runs in the race. He says, "Those who run in the race are all running, but one takes the reward. (1 Cor 9:24-27)

It may seem that disobeying God's will is not a serious matter, but it will turn out to be very dangerous when the Lord comes, and He tests our deeds, then it will be too late.

He says: "... knowing that you will receive from the Lord the reward of inheritance, but the oppressor will receive what he has done wrong, not favoritism." (Cor 3:24, 25)

3- Obedience to God's will: This is the correct position.

He says: "Instead of saying, 'If the Lord wills and we live, we will do this or that' (Jas 4:15). This statement is not for consumption but expresses the attitude of the heart of the believer. Jesus said, "My food is to do the will of Him who sent me and to do His work" (Jn 4:34).

"Whoever knows how to do well and does not do it is a sin for him" (Jas 4:17). Doing God's will express the existence of a vital relationship between God and the believer, and this relationship does not end when the believer disobeys. For the Father still treats us as children, even if it leads to him disciplining us. In God's will, we may suffer, we may be weak, but we do not die. God wants us to understand His will, not just to know it. (Eph 5:17).

We should experience God's will. He says, "Let you experience what is the good, pleasing and perfect will of God" (Rom 12:2).

We often ask: How do I know God's will for my life?
The answer is: Start with the thing you know you should do, and God opens the way to the next step as He completes.
The Lord Jesus says, "Take up my yoke upon you and learn from me" (Matthew 11:29). The yoke is meant to practice what we have learned from God in Scripture.

Finally, we have to do God's will from the heart.
He says, "Do the will of God from the heart" (Eph 6:6).
What the Apostle Paul said about giving also applies to life, as in this saying: "It is not about sorrow or compulsion." (2 Cor 9:7)

We obey God's will not because it is obligatory for us, but because we want to. The secret of happiness in the Christian life is to rejoice in the Lord as we walk with Him, then trials and sufferings turn to blessings.

What are the benefits we derive from doing God's will?

First, we enjoy deeper fellowship with Jesus Christ. Jesus said: "For he who does the will of God is my brother, my sister, and my mother" (Mk 3:35).

Second: We shall have the privilege of knowing the divine truth. "If anyone wills to do the will of God, he will know the teaching" (Jn 7:17)

Third: We experience the answer to Prayer.
"And this is the confidence that we have that if we ask for something according to His will, He will listen to us" (1 Jn 5:14)

Fourth: We wait for the reward at the end
"Come, blessed be my Father, and inherit the kingdom

prepared for you from the foundation of the world" (Matthew 25:34)

Chapter Five

Money speaks
The wage of the laborer screams
(James 5:1- 6)

And in this chapter the apostle James addresses the rich and says that they were using their wealth for selfish purposes, and that they were persecuting the poor.
It puts before us two thoughts:
1. The affliction in which the laborers that are deprived of the wages of their labors suffer, and they cry out unto God. He says: "Behold, the wages of the laborers who mowed your fields, which you kept back by fraud, are crying out against you, and the cry of the harvesters has reached the ears of The Lord of hosts" (Jas 5:4) And the distress that some other people are subjected to because of hardship and illness. He says: "is any one among you sick, let them call the elders to pray over them, and anoint them with oil in the name of the Lord" (Jas 5:13,14)

2- And the second thought is prayer
The wretched doers cry out to God, and the sick as well and

the distressed must pray. Elijah is mentioned as an example of those who believe in the power of prayer.
He says: "Elijah was a man under suffering like us and prayed a prayer that it would not rain, and it did not rain ... and he prayed again, and the sky gave rain..." (Jas 5:17, 18)
Thus, we come to the fifth characteristic of a mature believer, which is that he prays a lot in tribulations.

The mature believer turns to God by prayer, especially in times of trouble, to seek divine help. "Come now, rich men, weep for your coming misery" (Jas 5:1) James did not say that it is a sin to be rich. Abraham was rich, yet he walked with God, and God blessed him and blessed the world through him. But James speaks of the selfishness of the rich, and he advised them to weep and weep, for the following reasons:
1. The way in which the rich made their wealth (Jas 5:4, 6)
The acquisition of wealth illegally is unacceptable, and the Apostle James gave here two explanations, he said:

(1) Underestimate the wages of the laborers (Jas 5:4) They hired the laborers to do the work and did not give them the wage they deserved, which is agreed on.
The story of the labor mentioned in (Matthew 20:1-16) gives us an idea of the labor system of those days.
In (Deuteronomy 24:14, 15), he says: "Do not oppress a poor and poor wage earner from your brothers or from strangers in your land, in his day thou shalt give him his wages, and the sun shall not set upon them: for he is poor, and he needs it, lest he cry out against thee unto the Lord, and thou shalt have sin."

(2) They judged the righteous
He says, "You killed him, he will not resist you" (Jas 5:6).
It appears that they had political power, so they used their influence to get what they wanted. The golden rule says, "Whatever you want people to do to you, do so also to them" (Matthew 7:12). Perhaps the courts during James's time were so accessible that the rich controlled them.
He says: "You judged the righteous, you killed him, he will not

45

resist you" (Jas 5:6)
2. The way in which the rich used their wealth (Jas 5:3-5)
He says: "You have lived on earth in luxury and in self-indulgence ..." (Jas 5:5)
Obtaining wealth through injustice is terrible, but spending wealth in sin is even more terrible.

(1) They stored it:
They stored it at a time when these oppressed people needed the necessary sustenance. They wanted to become rich and thought that storing money in this way would make them become rich.
While the Lord Jesus says, "Treasure for you in heaven, where no mite or rust spoils, and where thieves do not dig up and they don't steal" (Mt 6:19)
History says that almost ten years after this letter was written, Jerusalem fell into the hands of the Romans and was plundered. Those riches that were stored, and those who stored them did not benefit from them.

(2) They have deprived the beneficiaries of their wages
"Behold, the wages of the laborers.... that are underestimated by you cry out" (Jas 5:4) Neither did the rich use their wealth, nor did they let the poor use it for their basic needs.
Because we are stewards of what God has given us, we therefore have responsibilities in Christian stewardship.
We should be faithful so that we use what God has given us for the benefit of others.
He says, "Then he will ask the stewards, that man may be found faithful" (1 Cor 4:2)
Joseph was faithful in the house of Potiphar (Gen 39).

(3) They lived in luxury:
"You have lived on earth in luxury and in self-indulgence" (Jas 5:5)
The Lord Jesus said, "Look and guard against greed, for when anyone has much, his life is not his money." (Luke

12:15) There is a big difference between enjoying what God has given us and living on what we have illegally taken from others.

He says: "I command the rich in the present age not to be arrogant and not to cast their hope on the uncertainty of riches, but on God, who richly gives us all things to enjoy" (1 Tim 6:17)
What has become of their wealth?

He says, "Weep for your coming misery" (Jas 5:1). This is how James described the consequences of the misuse of the rich, and he said:

(1) The richness will dissipate

"Your riches have worn out.... your gold and silver have rusted, ..." (Jas 5:2, 3)

It is a big mistake to think that there is security in wealth.
It is absurd to live for money, to devote time, effort, and life to it, because we cannot take something with us from it.
The Lord Jesus says, "And God said to him, you fool, this very night your life will be demanded from you, for who have you prepared this for?" (Lk 12:20)
Money in itself is not sin, but the love of money is the root of all evil. (1 Tim 6:10) And he says in (Ps 62:10): "If wealth increases, do not put a heart on it."

(2) Judgment is inevitable:

"... And the cry of the reapers has entered the ears of the LORD of hosts" (Jas 5:4) He says, "Your gold and silver are rusty, and their rust will be a testimony against you, and your flesh will be consumed like fire" (Jas 5:3). It is not only judgment in the present time (rust and fire), but judgment is also coming, and it will be before the Lord of hosts, who is fair. And there will be witnesses in the divine court, for the wealth of the rich will testify against them. Moths, rust, selfishness, understated wages, and also the laborers themselves. There is no room for changing the judiciary.

What will money say about us when it speaks on the last

day? God has heard the cry of the oppressed laborers and reapers, and there will be no opportunity to change the judiciary on that last day. The final judgment will be decisive, for the perishing will stand for judgment before Christ at the white throne (Rev 20:11-15). But the saved people will appear before the seat of Christ, and each of them will give an account of what he has done. (2 Cor 5:9, 10)

As believers, we will not be condemned for our sins, because Christ bore them for us on the cross, but we will be judged for our works and service. And we will be rewarded with crowns if we are faithful, but if we lose our crown, we will not lose our salvation. He says, "And the work of each man will be manifest, for the day will be revealed, for by fire he will be revealed, and the fire will test the work of each one. If there is any man's work left that he has built on, he will take a wage. If anyone's work is burned, he will lose, but he will be saved, but as with fire" (1 Cor 3:13-15).

He says, "You have treasured in the last days" (Jas 5:3). This indicates that the apostle James was expressing that the second coming of the Lord was near. The coming of the Lord is at hand. We have to spend time and work as long as it is day. It is good to have things that can be bought with money, but it is better to have things that cannot be bought with money. So, what good does a house that costs more than half a million dollars benefit us, when we are strangers and guests? And we do not have a homeland on earth?

The apostle James did not condemn the richness or the rich people, but he condemned the way in which the rich used their riches.

One of them said, "What we keep we lose, but what we give to the Lord we keep, and the Lord also adds to it."

The Power of Patience
(James 5:7-12)

" Therefore, brethren, wait for the coming of the Lord" (Jas 5:7) That is to say, be patient, which is the same counsel that he gave at the beginning of the letter (James 1:1-5).
We as believers must exercise patience. He says, "... with many tribulations, we must enter the kingdom of God" (Acts 14:22).

The apostle James used two words to express "patience" In (Jas 5:7, 8, 10) the expression is mentioned: Be patient, and he says: "Therefore, brethren, wait for the coming of the Lord." He waits for the precious fruit of the earth, careful about it ..." And in (Jas 5:10) he mentions another expression, which is endurance and patience, He says, "My brethren, take an example of endurance of hardship and patience, the prophets who spoke in the name of the Lord."

The words "endurance" and "patience" mean that the believer remains under load and pressure and continues to perform his work.

The Apostle James gives us three examples of patience and endurance:

1. The farmer (Jas 5:7-9):

"Behold, the farmer waits for the precious fruit of the earth, taking care of it until it receives the early and late rain" (Jas 5:7). Early rain softens the soil, and late rain comes in spring and helps crops ripen. The farmer has no authority over the weather, so he must be patient and endure. For the fruit of the earth is precious, and we wait, for "we shall reap in his time, if we do not tire" (Gal 6:9). And God wants from our lives a spiritual harvest, which is the fruit of the Spirit (Gal 5:22). And the way of suffering is the only way in whom the Lord bears fruit in our lives.

The Apostle James likens the believer to the farmer who waits for the harvest, saying: "So you be patient and firm your hearts, because the coming of the Lord is near" (James 5:8) Our hearts are the soil, and the seed is the Word of God. And we ought to work it out in us and have spiritual fruits. One of the qualities of a farmer is patience, and we are to surrender to the Lord and give room for the fruit to grow in our lives. He says, "be patient and stand firm with all your heart" (Jas 5:8). And to have a focused heart is the primary spiritual ministry of the believers in the church, the unstable heart cannot yield fruits.

Another characteristic of a farmer is that he is ready to help his neighbor, there is no time and no energy to waste in the conflict with his neighbors. He says, "Do not groan against one another, brethren, lest you be judged. Behold, the Judge stands at the door" (Jas 5:9).

2. The Prophets (Jas 5:10)

"Take for yourselves, brethren, the prophets, as an example of the endurance of hardship and suffering, the prophets who spoke in the name of the Lord" (Jas 5:10).
What encouragement do we benefit from this parable?

The prophets were in the will of God, they were ministering in the name of The Lord, and yet they suffered and got persecuted. Satan suggests to the faithful believer that his sufferings are the result of his sin and unfaithfulness, although it is the opposite, it is the result of his honesty and sincerity. The Bible says, "And those who want to live godly in Christ Jesus will be persecuted" (2 Tim 3:12)

It is better not to think that our obedience to God produces comfort and joy in the world, for Jesus was obedient, and this led Him to the cross.

The parable of the prophets also reminds us that God takes care of us when we enter into suffering. Like when God took care of Elijah against the wicked king Ahab, God took care of him in the time of drought, also supported him over the priests of Baal.

3. Job (Jas 5:11)

"Behold, we are blessed with patience, you have heard with the patience of Job, ..." (Jas 5:11)

How can we be patient without going through trials and tribulations? No victories without battles. If we seek blessing, we must take up the weapon of God and enter the spiritual battle. We cannot find a greater example of suffering than the one Job faced. All circumstances were against him, because he lost his wealth and health, lost his children dear to his heart, and his wife was against him, for she said to him, "Curse God and die" (Job 2:9). And his friends were also against him, because they accused him of hypocrisy, and that he deserved God's judgment.

And it also seemed like God Himself is against him too, when he cried out to God for an explanation of what had happened to him, he could not find an answer. And in all of this, he was patient and endured. But he found mercy from God, and he said, "By the ear I have heard of you, and now my eyes have seen you" (Job 42:5).

Why did the Apostle James tell the story of Job, and what does the story mean for believers these days?

It means that some temptation comes from demonic opposites. God allows Satan to tempt us, but He always limits his power so that he does not prevail over us. (Job 1:12), (Job 2:6).

When you find yourself in the fire, remember that God puts His hand on the thermostat, and He is ready to give you grace upon grace so that you can endure. Job says, "For he knows my way, if he tempts me, I will come out like gold" (Job 23:10).

One of the purposes of God's permitted suffering is the edification of character.

Job must have become a better person after he entered the furnace of trials.

The Power of Prayer
(James 5: 13-20)

Prayer is a great privilege for believers. As children of God, we can come to the throne of grace freely and courageously, and express to God our needs.

The mature believer prays a lot in tribulations.

In this chapter, the Apostle James encourages us to pray by offering four situations in which God responds to prayer:

1. Praying for those who are in trouble:

"Is anyone among you going through hardships, let them pray" (Jas 5:13)

What do we do when we find ourselves in difficult circumstances?

We should not complain or groan at others, as in (Jas 5:9), and we should not put the blame on the Lord, but we should pray, and we seek the wisdom we need to understand the situation and use it for the glory of God.

Prayer can relieve hardships, if this is God's will, and prayer also gives us greater grace (Jas 4:6) so that God might turn hardships into victories. When Paul prayed for the thorn in his body, God gave him grace, which he needed to turn his weakness into power (2 Corinthians 12). And the Lord Jesus prayed to the Heavenly Father in the Garden of Gethsemane to lift the cup from him, but the Father gave him the power that He needed it to go to the cross and die for our sins.

"Is anyone happy, let them sing songs of praise" (Jas 5:13)

God knows how to balance our lives; He gives us a hymn in the midst of our suffering. And the mature believer can sing praises during his suffering. The Bible says, "God brings songs at night" (Job 35:10). And this is what happened with Paul and Silas in Philippians prison, as in (Acts 16:25).

Our hymn must be an expression of our spiritual life, which comes out of the heart and is motivated by the Holy Spirit. It must be based on the Word of God, not on people's thoughts.

2. Praying for the sick:

"If anyone is sick among you, let him call the elders of the church, and pray over him, and anoint him with oil in the name of the Lord, and the prayer of faith heals the sick and the Lord raises him up, even if he has committed a sin, he will be forgiven" (Jas 5:14, 15)

James describes the sick person for whom prayer is intended as:

(1) Sick because of sin (Jas 5:15)

He says: "... And if he has done a sin, he will be forgiven" (Jas 5:15).

The original text says, "If he constantly sins."

This corresponds to what it says in (1 Cor 11:30), where it says: "For this reason there are many among you who are weak and sick, and many who die"

(2) He must confess his sins:

He says, "Confess to one another the trespasses, pray for one another that you may be healed" (Jas 5:16).

(3) Healing by the Prayer of Faith:

"And the prayer of faith heals the sick, and the Lord raises him up" (Jas 5:15). It is not the oil that heals, but the prayer of faith. The prayer of faith is what the Apostle John said: "This is the trust that we have in him, that if we ask for something according to His will, He hears us, and if we know that whatever we ask, he will hear us, we know that we have the requests that we have asked of him" (1 Jn 5:14)

He says, "if we confess our sins, He is faithful and just so that He forgives our sins" (1 Jn 1:9) And we also confess to those to whom we have sinned against, saying, "confess to one another trespasses" (James 5:16).

3. Praying for the nation:
In (Jas 5:17, 18), the apostle James gave an example of Elijah as one who believes in the power of prayer.
And James says that Elijah was a man under suffering like us, and he prayed for his nation, and the Lord answered him. And the story says that God punished the nation by stopping the rain that the earth needs for three and a half years. (Deuteronomy 28:12, 23) Then it became dry, and the earth could not produce the food necessary for life.
Then Elijah challenged the priests of Baal on Mount Carmel. The priests prayed to their gods all day, and it was in vain. But Elijah repaired the altar and offered the sacrifice, and prayed once, and the fire came down from heaven and ate the offering. And he also prayed for the rain, and the LORD answered, and the sky rained, and the earth was watered.
He says, "Elijah was a man under suffering like us" (Jas 5:17). This is so that no one thinks that God answered Elijah's prayer, and he does not respond to anyone else.
Elijah was a prophet, but he was under suffering like us, and he was not perfect. After his victory over Mount Carmel, he was afraid, fled, and hid. But he was a righteous man, in the sense that he was obedient to God. God promised to answer the prayer of all his faithful children who are called by his name.
Prayer is power, and the power of prayer is the greatest power in the world today. Elijah prayed for his nation, and the Lord answered him. And we need to pray for the world today, so that the Lord sends a revival to the church. And to pray for leaders in the world, to do God's will.

4. Praying for the lost:
"If any of you strayed from the truth, let anyone who return

him, let him know that whoever turns a sinner away from the straying of his path will save a soul from death." (James 5:19)

The word "astray" means astray away from the truth, and sometimes the brother falls into a slip and says: "Brothers, if someone is caught in a sin, and he took in a slip, you who are spiritual should restore him gently (Gal 6:1)

And this man who has gone astray poses a danger to the church, so he can be a stumbling block to others, and affect the immature, so they do like him he says, "... but one sinner will corrupt a great good" (Ja 9:18). That is why we invite the spiritual brothers and sisters of the Church to help the man who has lost his way. He says, "If any one among you strayed from the truth" (Jas 5:19).

And the truth is the Word of God. And the Lord Jesus warned Peter that Satan would tempt him, but Peter did not believe the word, but rather he was arguing with the Lord. And at the time when he should have prayed, he fell asleep, it is not surprising that he denied the Lord three times also.

And if we want to help the brother who has gone astray, we need to have enough love. He says, "For love covers up many sins" (1 Pet 4:8).

He says: "In (Jas 5:20): "Whoever brings a sinner back from his wandering, will save his soul from death and
covers a multitude of sins."

The Apostle James and the Apostle Peter learned this principle from the Book of Proverbs, where he says: "Hatred stirth up strifes, but love covers all sins" (Prov 10:12) Love also helps the lost to face his sins and assures him that there is forgiveness.

Questions for review:

1. Who is the author of the Epistle of James? Why did he write his letter?

2. What is the subject of the letter? What are the signs that show the spiritual maturity of the believer?

3. Why does the apostle James regard temptations as a cause for joy?

4. How can we deal with temptation and overcome it?

5. What does the apostle James mean by saying, "Do not deceive your souls?"

6. What is the thought of the Apostle James on the subject of differentiation in the treatment of rich and poor?

7. Do you understand what is meant by the expression "law of freedom" and also "royal law"? And what did you understand?

8. The Apostle James made a comparison between dead faith and active faith; can you explain that?

9. Is a man saved by faith or by works? How do you explain that?

10. Who is the perfect man in the eyes of the apostle James? Why?

11. Explain in focused phrases why the apostle James considers the tongue to be a cause of destruction?

12. Write in your own style an explanation of the meaning of human wisdom, and is it true or false?

13. How can you distinguish between true wisdom and false wisdom?

14. What is the meaning of the verse that says, "And the fruit of righteousness shall be sown in peace by those who do peace"?

15. Why does war arise within our souls? What are its results?

16. How can a believer declare war against God? Illustrate in brief points.

17. What are the three directions that the apostle James gives us to renew our relationship with God?

18. Why did James emphasize the importance of prayer?

19. How did the rich offend the poor workers? Why did they do that?

20. The apostle James gave three examples of patience, which he spoke briefly.

Printed by Amazon Italia Logistica S.r.l.
Torrazza Piemonte (TO), Italy